## WHEN MEN PANNED GOLD IN THE KLONDIKE

color, excitement, and suspense filled their days, for no one knew who might be next to strike it rich. As much as $20,000 worth of gold was sometimes mined in a single day, and many men became millionaires practically overnight. Many more found only disappointment following their stampede to the Klondike region of Canada's Yukon Territory.

The hope of instant riches drove more than 22,000 people to make the long, difficult trip to the gold fields by train, ship, and finally on foot. The flavor of that frantic search for gold is captured in this exciting account. The colorful characters whose lives were a part of this story come to life again. Old photographs and fresh new drawings done especially for this book vividly enhance the text.

This book is one of the *How They Lived* Series, developed by Garrard to give meaning to the study of American history. Young people will find a deeper understanding and a more lasting appreciation of history and geography as they see life in the past through the eyes of those who lived it.

When Men Panned Gold in the Klondike

# When Men Panned Gold in the Klondike

BY EDWARD C. JANES

ILLUSTRATED BY WILLIAM HUTCHINSON

GARRARD PUBLISHING COMPANY
CHAMPAIGN, ILLINOIS

## Picture credits:

All the black and white photographs which illustrate this book were taken from 1897 to 1904 by E. A. Hegg and other pioneer photographers. These brave men packed their equipment over dangerous mountain passes and down the Yukon River to leave a lasting record of the great Klondike gold rush.

# Contents

# 1. Gold!

On a hot August afternoon in 1896, George Washington Carmack trudged along the bank of a small stream called Rabbit Creek, in the Yukon. With him were two of his Indian friends, Skookum Jim and Tagish Charlie. The three men were looking for gold. They had searched for this precious yellow metal, from time to time, all the way from Juneau, Alaska, to the headwaters of the mighty Yukon River and along the Klondike River. But, so far, they had found no gold.

They knew that the best place to look for gold is along the banks of streams. This is because running water washes gold from the rocks that hold the mother lode, or the main supply. Gold is often found right in the beds of streams, but the largest amounts are usually buried deep under earth and sand along the banks.

Some of it is washed away in tiny specks like dust. Other pieces are as large as gravel or are nuggets the size of small stones. Because the smallest pieces are lightest, they are carried farther by the water. So when miners find gold dust, they go upstream looking for the larger pieces.

Not all places have gold in the ground, but Alaska does. Alaska is a huge, sprawling land of forests, mountains, rivers, and wildlife, which is part of the United States. It used to be inhabited mostly by Eskimos and Indians. For many years only a few white men lived in Alaska. Then gold was discovered. As the first rumors trickled into the United States and Canada, dozens of adventurous men hurried to Alaska to search for more gold.

Some had found gold near Juneau, Alaska, and a town grew up there. Others had followed the Yukon River into the Klondike region of Yukon Territory, which belongs to Canada.

Even before 1896, miners had roamed the valleys of Alaska and Yukon Territory searching for gold.

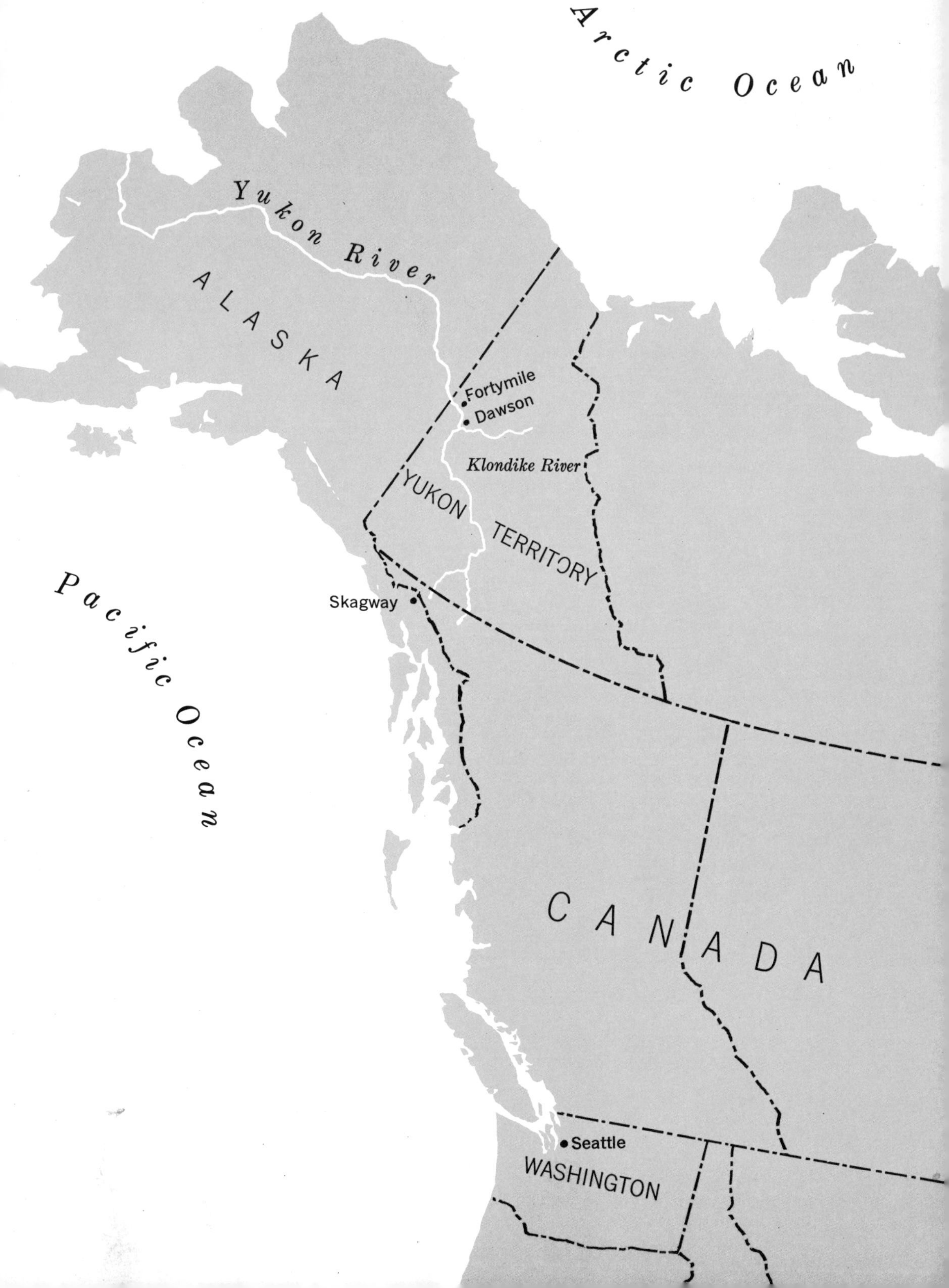
Arctic Ocean
Yukon River
ALASKA
Fortymile
Dawson
Klondike River
YUKON
TERRITORY
Skagway
Pacific Ocean
CANADA
Seattle
WASHINGTON

They had found a little gold, here and there, but no large amounts had been discovered. And George Carmack, Skookum Jim, and Tagish Charlie had found no gold at all.

On this August afternoon as they plodded along beside Rabbit Creek, they were wet with perspiration because the sun was hot and the trail was rough. Clouds of mosquitoes swarmed about them as they fought their way through briars and raspberry canes and floundered over moss-grown fallen trees. They wore moccasins, frayed corduroy trousers, red flannel shirts, and battered broad-brimmed hats. They carried knapsacks, blankets, axes, rifles, and tin cooking and eating utensils. Each man also carried a small pick and shovel and a broad, shallow pan. These were the tools that every miner used in looking for gold.

In the late afternoon they came to a fork in the creek. Here, tired from their long day, they set up camp for the night. Tagish Charlie began to chop a fallen spruce into firewood. Skookum Jim set out with his rifle to shoot some game for supper.

There are two stories of what happened then. One is that George Carmack went to the creek for a kettle of water. As he dipped the kettle

This prospector patiently pans for gold in a shallow Klondike creek. When sand and mud are washed away, gold may be left at the bottom of the pan.

into the clear mountain stream, his roving eyes
fell upon a lump of glistening yellow metal
in the shallow water at his feet. Reaching out
with suddenly trembling fingers, he picked it
up. He knew at once that he had found a
nugget of gold. With a great shout he ran
back to the camp.

"Gold!" he cried and showed Tagish Charlie
the lump he had found in the stream bed.

Skookum Jim, who had heard Carmack's
shout, hurried back from his hunting and he,
too, stared at the lump of gleaming metal.
Carmack grabbed his shovel and pan and
raced back to the creek bank. Skookum Jim
and Tagish Charlie followed at his heels. Anx-
iously they watched as Carmack shoveled a
scoop of mud and gravel into his broad pan.
Then, holding the pan under water, he began
shaking it with a circular motion of his hand.

Gradually the sand and fine gravel washed
away over the side of his round pan. At last
there was left a fine sprinkling of yellow dust
which, being heavier than the sand and gravel,
had sunk to the bottom of the pan. In this
one panful of dirt there was a quarter of an
ounce of gold worth about four dollars. Carmack flung down the pan with a war whoop

in which his Indian friends joined as they all danced upon the bank of Rabbit Creek.

Then Carmack went to work once more, filling his pan with gravel and washing it away until he had enough coarse gold to fill an empty shotgun shell. Only then did the three return to their camp.

The other story tells us that it was Skookum Jim who found the gold. He and Tagish Charlie later claimed that George Carmack was asleep under a shady tree when Skookum Jim went out to shoot game. They said that Jim shot a moose and then went to the creek to clean a dishpan. While he was cleaning the pan, he found the gold nugget. No one knows for sure which story is true. But Carmack always called himself the discoverer of gold in the Klondike. And most people agree.

Early next morning Carmack paced off 250 feet along the stream on each side of the spot where the gold had been found. Then he chipped the bark from a small spruce tree beside the stream at the lower end of the ground he had measured. With the stub of a pencil he wrote on the trunk:

> To Whom It May Concern
> I do, this day, locate and claim by right of discovery, five hundred feet running upstream from this notice. Located this 17th day of August, 1896.
>
> G. W. Carmack

This is called staking a claim. Sometimes miners did it by driving stakes in the ground at each end of their chosen territory and writing on the stakes. At other times they staked claims as Carmack had.

Since the land where Carmack had found the gold was in the Yukon Territory of Canada, he had to follow Canadian laws. These allowed only one claim for each person, except for the discoverer of the gold, who could stake two claims. Also, by the laws of Canada, Carmack's claim ran along both sides of the stream.

Below it, he staked another claim for himself as discoverer. Then below his second claim he measured and staked off another claim for Tagish Charlie. This claim was called Two Below, and Skookum Jim's claim, which Carmack staked above his original claim, was called One Above. And that was how claims were always

This photograph taken after gold miners began to dig shows the area where Carmack first staked his claim.

numbered and named in Canada. Each claim was 500 feet long.

When Carmack had finished, he and his friends set out for the nearest town, Forty-mile, to have their claims written down in the record book there. First they hiked about fifteen miles down Rabbit Creek to the place where it flowed into the Klondike River. This was the worst part of the trip. Once again they had to flounder through prickly briars and wade knee-deep through swamps. Mosquitoes swarmed around them and in the hot August sun the men were soaked with perspiration. Now, though, they were so excited about the gold they had found that, as they hurried along, they scarcely noticed the briar scratches, the clouds of insects, or the hot sun.

In the late afternoon they fought their way out of the brush and found a canoe, which they had hidden near the mouth of the Klondike River. As they carried it to the water's edge, they saw four men poling a loaded boat up the river. Carmack shouted to them, beckoning them to come ashore. As they drew near, he held up the shell full of gold dust.

"Gold!" he shouted. "Gold!"

The four men grounded their boat on the

16

shore and leaped out. When they saw Carmack's gold, their eyes nearly popped out of their heads. They were from Nova Scotia and had been searching for gold for months. Now they were on their way up the Klondike River to try their luck once more.

"Wh.. where did you find that?" the leader, David McKay, stammered.

"About fifteen miles up Rabbit Creek," Carmack replied, for it was an unwritten law among miners to share their good fortune with others. "Just keep on up the creek and you'll see where our claims are staked."

Hardly stopping to thank him, the four men dragged their boat into the bushes. Grabbing their shovels, pans, and knapsacks, they set out at almost a run along the bank of Rabbit Creek. This chance meeting with Carmack made fortunes for all of them.

George Carmack, Tagish Charlie, and Skookum Jim made camp that night a few miles down the Klondike River where darkness overtook them. Early the next morning they were on their way again. About noon they saw two men cooking their lunch on a sandbar where the Klondike River flows into the Yukon. They went ashore to join them. These men were

French-Canadians who had been looking for gold for months. Now, discouraged and almost out of food, they were returning to Fortymile.

"If I were you, I wouldn't go back to Fortymile yet," Carmack told them. "Maybe this will change your minds." He showed them his gold. "I found it up Rabbit Creek and there's plenty more for both of you."

Carmack gave the astounded men some food, and the last he saw of them, they were poling furiously up the river, bound for Rabbit Creek. Jim went back to Rabbit Creek to guard the claims, while Carmack and Tagish Charlie continued on the trip to Fortymile.

18

In midafternoon Carmack and his companion
came in sight of a little cluster of log cabins.
This was the town of Fortymile, perched on a
bluff overlooking the Yukon River. Here they
landed and started to the police station to have
their claims registered in the record book. To
each person whom he met on the way, Carmack cried: "Follow me! I've got something to
show you."

By the time he and Tagish Charlie reached
the police station, a group of curious people
straggled at their heels asking one another
what was going on. Carmack strode into the
recorder's office and leaned against the counter,

as his little band of followers pressed through the door.

"Folks," he said, "I've got good news for you. I've found gold on Rabbit Creek. There are millions of dollars worth of it there waiting to be dug out of the ground. So get up there in a hurry!"

Some of them refused to believe Carmack until he showed them the gold. Then, like magic, the news spread through Fortymile. *Gold! Rabbit Creek!* Men and women came running from their cabins to see Carmack's gold and to hear the story of its discovery. A big crowd gathered around the police station. Everyone was talking at once, asking questions, and shouting the news.

Soon, singly and in groups, men began to leave town. The next morning hardly a man remained in Fortymile. By boat and on foot they were all hurrying to stake claims along Rabbit Creek. From Fortymile the news spread throughout the Yukon Valley as one person told another. News of the discovery finally reached Alaska in January. Men from Juneau and Skagway, from Sitka and Dyea, and from all of Alaska now began to swarm into the area. The great Klondike gold rush had begun.

## 2. Big Alex Builds a Cabin

By the fall of 1896, the entire length of
Rabbit Creek was changed. The briar roses
and raspberry canes through which George
Carmack and his friends had fought their way
had been cleared from the trampled, muddy
ground. Stumps showed where trees had been
cut for firewood or chopped to build the log
cabins which now lined both sides of the little
creek. Even its name had been changed from
Rabbit Creek to Bonanza Creek, a name that
comes from a Spanish word meaning success.

The small branch, which formed the fork and had never had a name before, was now called Eldorado Creek. This name comes from the Spanish word for golden. It was well named, for Eldorado Creek turned out to be even richer in gold than Bonanza. Within weeks of Carmack's discovery, claims had been staked from one end to the other of both streams, and miners were hard at work.

One of the men who had come to Eldorado Creek was "Big Alex" McDonald. He was a

Prospectors who poured into the Yukon began to pan for gold as soon as they had staked their claims.

This miner scrubs his weekly laundry in front of his
tent. Most newly-arrived prospectors lived in tents.

tall, broad-shouldered miner with a thick mop
of black hair and a great handle-bar mustache.
Later he was to be known as "The King of
the Klondike," for his claim, Number Thirty
Above, and the shares he owned in other claims
brought him over five million dollars.

When he arrived in October, ice was already
beginning to form along the creek banks, and
geese were flying south in swift V's before the
approaching Arctic winter. Like most miners
when they first arrived, he lived in a tent. But
he knew there was no time to lose in building
a snug cabin. Some of the other men had partners to help them build their cabins and mine
the gold, but Big Alex was alone. He was what
the miners called a "lone wolf."

Big Alex had to go some distance back from the creek to find logs for his cabin because most of the nearby trees had already been cut down earlier by others. But he didn't mind, for he was as strong as a moose. Selecting tall spruce trees about seven inches through, he chopped them down and cut them into logs, sixteen feet long for the ends of his cabin, and eighteen feet long for the sides.

He dragged them one by one to the spot he had cleared beside his claim. Then he carefully flattened a three-inch strip along the top and bottom of each log so that the logs would lie close together when they were placed upon one another. He had only a sharp ax and a saw for tools. Since nails and spikes were very scarce and expensive, he fastened the logs together at the corners by cutting notches in the ends to fit them into one another.

First he laid two logs for the sides on the ground in their proper positions. Then he placed the logs for the ends across them, fitting the notches together to form a rectangle. Then he spread a three-inch layer of moss over the top of this frame before placing more logs on top of the first ones. The moss was used to fill any cracks between the logs and to make

24

A light snowfall warns miners that they must finish
this cabin before the bitter Klondike winter begins.

the walls tighter. Well-built walls would keep
out the mosquitoes in summer and the icy
winds in winter.

Each day he added more logs and moss while
the ring of other men's axes and the rasp of
their saws echoed around him. Some were
putting the finishing touches on their cabins
and some were just beginning to build. The
smoky smell of bonfires hung in the air as men
burned brush in their clearings. Sometimes
they paused in their work to call back and
forth to each other.

Every day new men appeared along the
creek. They were tanned, bearded prospectors

25

looking for a place to stake claims in this rich new field. They stopped a moment to talk of gold and to spread the news they had brought from far-off settlements downriver. Then they hurried on, anxious to stake claims of their own.

Big Alex kept on working. His claim had shown large amounts of gold right near the surface of the ground, and no one knew what he might find when he dug down to the vein of gold called the pay streak. But first the cabin must be finished.

He cut openings for a door and two windows and piled on more logs and moss until the walls stood seven feet high. Now he was ready to place a big log called a ridgepole from one end of the cabin to the other, about five feet above the walls. To prop up this beam, he slanted poles from the walls to the ridge and covered them with a thick layer of earth and moss.

There was no glass for the windows, so he placed pieces of scraped reindeer skin across the openings. Then he made a door. Now all that remained was to build a rough plank table, two or three stools, and a bunk. The bunk was a sort of shallow box about fourteen feet long and four feet wide, built across one end of the cabin. It was filled with straw and moss for a mattress. A crossboard in the center divided the long box into two separate beds.

Big Alex had a sheet-iron stove, as did most of the miners, but he knew it would not warm the cabin in winter when the temperature fell to 60 degrees below zero. So he hollowed out a spot in the center of the dirt floor for a fireplace and cut a small opening in the roof to let out the smoke.

Now the cabin was finished, and Big Alex moved from his tent into his new home. He was just in time. That very night the first

Miners eat their scanty evening meal from a crudely set table. Food was so scarce during the winter of 1897-98 that many miners almost starved.

winter storm put snow on the ground. But inside his log house Big Alex was warm and cozy.

He had mixed a piece of sourdough—a fermented dough that causes bread to rise—with some flour, bacon fat, salt, and water to make himself some tasty loaves. Alaskan miners treasured their sourdough and kept lumps of it fermenting at all times, so that they could have homemade bread whenever they pleased. For this reason, they themselves were called sourdoughs.

Now Big Alex put his loaves in the oven. While they were baking, he fried bacon and boiled some beans on the top of his sheet-iron stove. When his meal was ready, he poured a mug of tea from the kettle beside the fireplace. Fierce gusts of wind howled around the cabin as he ate, but Big Alex did not care. Snug in his new home, he was safe from snow and cold.

# 3. Thomas Lippy's Gold Mine

One of Big Alex's neighbors was Thomas Lippy. He had been a YMCA instructor in Seattle. With his young wife he had come north to look for gold and had staked a claim, Number Sixteen Above, on Eldorado Creek.

As soon as he had finished building a cabin for himself and his wife, he began to dig the gold from his claim. It was very hard to do. The rich vein of gold known as the pay streak usually lay buried 20 or 30 feet deep in the earth. And in the Yukon, where temperatures

Klondike miners use their picks in cramped quarters
underground to dig toward the pay streak.

sometimes drop to 60 degrees below zero in
winter, the ground never thaws more than two
feet down, even in summer. Shovels and pick-
axes cannot dent it.

The only way Tom Lippy and the other
miners could dig a hole to reach the pay streak
was to melt the dirt first. To do this, they
built huge fires in the early evening and let
them burn all night. By the next morning the
fires had thawed the ground under them to a
depth of about six inches.

During the day Tom Lippy patiently dug out
the melted dirt until he came to the next layer

30

of frozen ground. At night he built another fire in the same place and the next day he dug out more dirt and rocks. In this way, after several weeks, he finally had a hole twenty feet deep and about four feet across. Miners call this hole a shaft. By now the shaft was so deep that Lippy could not throw out the dirt with his shovel. He had to build a hoisting device called a windlass which has a bucket on the end of a rope. He would go down the shaft, fill the bucket with dirt, and haul it up by pulling on the rope.

A miner works a windlass to bring a bucket of dirt up the shaft from the pay streak far below.

Each night Tom Lippy washed a little of the dirt in a big washtub of water, which he kept in his cabin. Putting some dirt in his broad miner's pan, he held the pan under water. Then he shook it with a circular motion, just as George Carmack had done the day he discovered gold on Rabbit Creek. When the dirt had washed away, Tom Lippy found gold dust in his pan. He knew then that he was nearing the pay streak.

On the fifteenth of December he found the rich vein of gold. Now, instead of digging his shaft deeper, he began to dig a tunnel to the

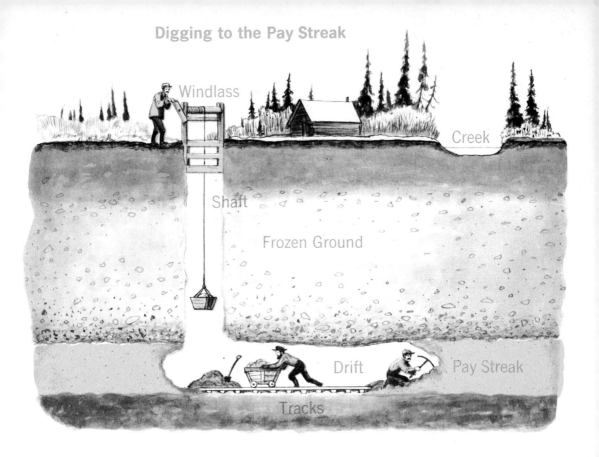

side, to follow the pay streak. This is called drifting. As his tunnel grew longer, he laid two wooden tracks on the dirt floor. He built a little cart to run on the tracks. He had to fill the cart with dirt and push it to the shaft. Then he shoveled the dirt into his bucket and hoisted it to the surface with his windlass. It was hard, tiring work. Of course, it was very dark in the tunnel, and he had to have a candle for light. It was fastened to the dirt wall of the tunnel.

33

Each week, as Tom Lippy continued drifting, the amount of gold left in the pan grew larger. The first panfuls of dirt had about $20 worth of gold in them. At the end of a couple of weeks, each panful had about $50 worth of gold. After a month of digging, Tom Lippy began washing out $100 or more to the pan.

He still had to build a fire each night to thaw the frozen dirt in the tunnel. And he still had to wash a few panfuls of dirt each night to be sure he was following the pay streak. The gold he washed out at night gave him enough money to buy groceries and supplies at the new town of Dawson, more than ten miles away at the mouth of the Klondike River.

While Thomas Lippy dug in his mine, his wife, Salome, was busy doing housework. She swept the cabin floor with a broom made of birch twigs. She dusted with a duster made of ptarmigan feathers. She made up the bunks with feather beds of goose down. Every day she baked sourdough bread in the sheet-iron stove.

Sometimes she put on her snowshoes and walked one mile through the snow to visit her neighbor, Mrs. Berry. Clarence Berry owned claim Number Six Above on Eldorado Creek. He had traded a claim on Bonanza Creek to a man named Antone Stander for his new claim on Eldorado. When he reached the pay streak, his mine proved to be very rich. For spending money, Mrs. Berry would take a stick and break up frozen chunks of mud that Clarence Berry had shoveled from his mine. In these chunks she often found gold nuggets. One afternoon she picked up $50 worth of gold in ten minutes!

All winter Tom Lippy worked in the smoky darkness of his mine. By spring he had dug a huge pile of dirt. The pile was so big that he could no longer wash it by hand. So now he set to work building some sluice boxes. A sluice box was a trough twelve feet long and ten inches wide with open ends. It had slats about one inch wide and ten feet long placed lengthwise along the bottom. It also had small strips of wood placed crosswise every two or three feet. He set several of these boxes on a slant under a little waterfall on Eldorado Creek so that water would flow through them very rapidly. The lower end of each box fitted tightly into the top end of another box. Together, they were called a sluice line.

Miners toss pay dirt into the swiftly running water in the sluice line. Mountains of discarded dirt and rocks surround them.

Then he began shoveling dirt from his huge pile into one end of the sluice line. The sand and dirt washed away, but the heavier gold sank to the bottom. Soon it lay thick and yellow between the wooden strips. When the space between the strips was filled, he moved the sluice line away from the waterfall and cleaned out the gold. He put it into buckskin bags, gold dust in one sack, nuggets in another.

Summer came and birds sang in the leafy trees. Tom Lippy still shoveled dirt into the sluice boxes and cleaned out the gold. When he had finished and there was no dirt left, he found that he had taken more than $100,000 worth of gold from his mine in the first year. Some other miners had grown rich, too. Big Alex McDonald had dug $94,000 worth of gold from number Thirty Above in one month. Clarence Berry took $130,000 from his mine. Up and down Bonanza and Eldorado Creeks were men who had been poor the year before. Now they were rich.

And all this time, no one in the United States had yet heard about the rich Klondike gold strike, since there was no telephone or telegraph in Alaska to carry the news.

Both dirt and water are shoveled into these rockers. As a miner cradles the rocker from side to side, the gold dust is washed through a screen to a tray below.

# 4. Chilkoot Lockstep

In the summer of 1897 some of the men who had made fortunes in the Klondike sailed home to the United States. With them they brought valises, cases, and bags, filled with gold. When they left the ship at Seattle, people near the wharf saw them struggle ashore with this heavy baggage.

"Gold!" someone shouted. "They're bringing gold!"

Gold! The word and the story of the arrival of the Klondike millionaires spread rapidly throughout the city. Over telegraph wires the news flashed from the Pacific Coast to the Atlantic Coast and over the cables to Europe. Soon the whole world knew about the gold strikes on Bonanza and Eldorado Creeks. Immediately a great wave of excitement swept all across the United States. Everyone talked about the gold, and thousands of people made plans to go to the gold fields.

Doctors, lawyers, teachers, farmers, factory workers, and clerks gave up their jobs to become miners. Most of them knew nothing about gold mining. They thought they could become millionaires just by staking a claim

Gold rushers with their supplies wait in Seattle for a steamship to take them north.

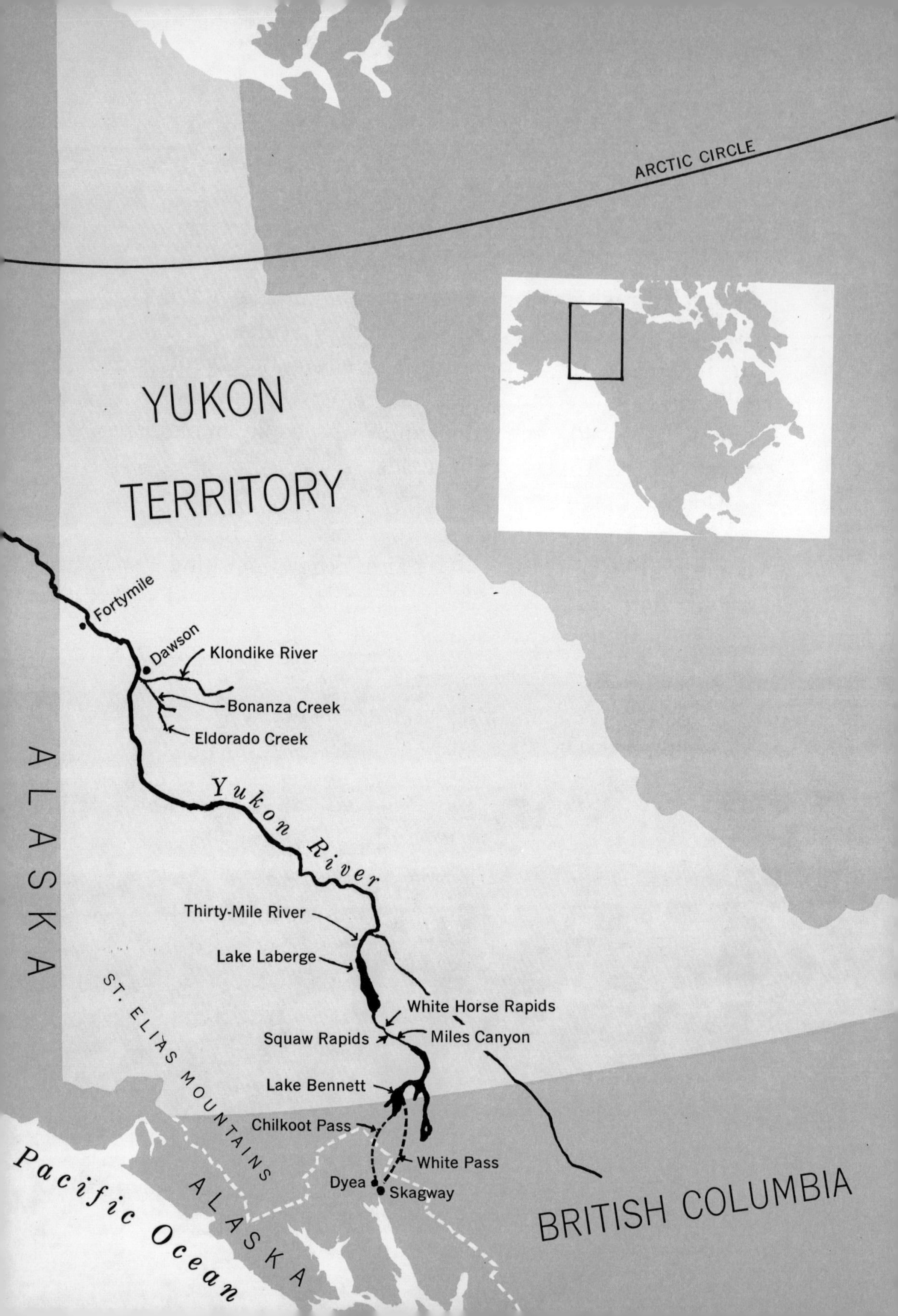

ARCTIC CIRCLE

YUKON

TERRITORY

ALASKA

Fortymile

Dawson

Klondike River

Bonanza Creek

Eldorado Creek

Yukon River

Thirty-Mile River

Lake Laberge

White Horse Rapids

Squaw Rapids

Miles Canyon

Lake Bennett

Chilkoot Pass

White Pass

Dyea

Skagway

ST. ELIAS MOUNTAINS

ALASKA

Pacific Ocean

BRITISH COLUMBIA

and digging a hole in the ground. Old sour-dough miners laughed when they heard this and called these new gold-seekers *cheechakos*, an Indian word meaning greenhorns.

Special trains carried crowds of *cheechakos* to San Francisco, or to Seattle in Washington. Every ship that could be used took them north from these ports to Skagway in Alaska.

The steamers dumped men and baggage on the Skagway beach until the shore looked like a giant anthill. A city of tents sprang up along the beach. Log cabins served as restaurants, stores, and shops. Men swarmed through the single muddy street, buying horses and food and mining equipment to take with them to the gold fields.

From Skagway they still had 700 miles to travel before reaching the Klondike. People with money could sail up the Yukon River by boat. But most of the *cheechakos* were too poor for this. They could follow a trail over White Pass through the St. Elias mountains to Lake Bennett, 40 miles away, and build boats there to take them on. Or they could reach Lake Bennett over the Chilkoot Pass from Dyea, a small town a few miles northwest of the port of Skagway.

*Cheechakos* made their way to the gold fields over dangerous mountain passes and down the treacherous Yukon River.

Many of them chose the trail over White Pass. This trail led through swamps and woods. It snaked over high mountains and across deep valleys. But by October, 1897, there was an endless procession of men and horses slowly climbing up the White Pass trail.

It was so steep and narrow in places that everyone had to stay in line. To make things worse, mosquitoes swarmed in clouds over men and horses. Sometimes the line had to stop for hours when an accident occurred ahead. Horses fell from the rocks and were killed. Still others were drowned in the swift rivers. So many died that this path became

Men and horses begin the climb over White Pass.

known as the Dead Horse Trail. Five thousand men and three thousand horses started through the White Pass in 1897, but only a few of the horses lived to reach Lake Bennett.

The Chilkoot Trail was much shorter than the White Pass. It ran through the same mountains but at a higher point. Because it was too steep for horses, the men had to carry all their supplies on their backs. They could hire Indians to help them. These Indians were short and stocky and very strong. They could easily carry loads of 150 pounds or more. But they charged about 40 cents a pound, and sometimes they would stop in the middle of the trail and demand more money.

By law, every man had to bring enough equipment and provisions to last him for a year. These weighed about a ton, or 2,000 pounds, and hiring Indians to carry them would cost $800. So most men lugged their own equipment, a little at a time. A man would carry from 50 to 100 pounds for a few miles. Then he would put down that load and go back down the trail for another load.

It took two or three months for a man to carry all his baggage over the Chilkoot Pass. People threw away things like trunks and

*Cheechakos* camp amidst the clutter of supplies and tents in Sheep Camp, first stop on Chilkoot Trail.

framed pictures and even jewelry which they did not really need. Both sides of this trail were littered with such belongings.

The trail led first to Sheep Camp at the foot of the mountain. Here there was a little town of tents and log cabins. Some of the log houses served as hotels. One, called the Palmer House, fed 500 people each day. The owner charged $2.50 for a plate of beans and bacon and a cup of weak tea. Forty people slept there every night. Since there were no beds, they all slept jammed together on the plank floor.

From Sheep Camp the trail climbed steeply to The Scales, a flat ledge where scales were kept and everything was weighed. From here to the summit the Indians charged a dollar a pound. Thousands of tons of supplies lay at The Scales, half-buried in the drifting snow. From morning till night a line of weary, struggling men and women trudged up the trail. Their backs were bent from their heavy loads. Their steaming breath came in gasps.

From The Scales to the summit was the steepest of all. Steps had been chopped in the ice on this part of the trail. Here the line moved slowly in a sort of shuffling gait that came to be called the "Chilkoot lockstep." It

This ant-like line of gold rushers carrying supplies struggles toward the summit of Chilkoot Pass.

took six hours to climb 1,000 feet with a 50-pound pack. When a man finally reached the top he laid down his pack and slid back to The Scales on the seat of his pants to get another load of supplies.

Most men could make only one trip a day, so it took 40 days to tote 2,000 pounds to the summit. It snowed almost all the time and some people got sick from being wet, half-

This *cheechako* is preparing to slide down to Sheep Camp to get another load.

frozen, and tired. But 22,000 men and women climbed over the Chilkoot Pass in 1897.

The Royal Canadian Northwest Mounted Police had a hut on the Canadian boundary line at the summit. The policemen saw many strange sights as they checked the thousands of *cheechakos* filing past their station. They saw lithe Indian girls with 75-pound packs on their backs. They saw a German woman, 70 years old, wearing her best dress and lace apron. They saw a man carrying a bicycle over the trail. And they saw a woman pulling a sled with a glowing stove on it. Whenever she stopped to rest, she could warm her hands and cook a meal.

Seventy feet of snow fell on the summit that year. One day the deep snow crumbled into an avalanche that swept more than 60 people to their deaths. But in spite of the snow, the cold, and the dangers, these determined men and women plodded on toward their goal. Ahead lay the gold fields where they hoped to become rich.

# 5. Rapids and Wrecks

Will Haskell had never seen such a sight in his life. For the past three months he and his partner, Joseph Meeker, had been packing their 4,000 pounds of equipment and supplies over the Chilkoot Pass. Now, at last, on a cold April day they stood on the shore of frozen Lake Bennett. All around the big lake, as far as they could see, stretched a huge tent city. Besides the tents in which people lived, there were tents for bakeries and tents for hot baths. There were barber tents, post office tents, and church tents.

In between the tents were heaped the mountains of freight which tired *cheechakos* had wrestled over the Dead Horse Trail and Chilkoot Pass. And almost everywhere they looked, men were building boats to take them the rest of the way to the Klondike.

The year before, Will Haskell and Joseph Meeker had been prospecting in Colorado. When they heard the news of the rich gold strike on Bonanza and Eldorado Creeks, they had joined the thousands of others bound for the Yukon. Now they still had a 500-mile journey by water before they reached the gold fields. They would have to wait until the ice melted from the lake to go on. While they waited, they built themselves a boat, as the others were doing.

There were very few expert boat builders at Lake Bennett. Most people just hammered boards together in the form of a boat which they hoped would float. The boats they built were of all shapes and sizes. Some were rafts, some were big, flat-nosed scows. Some were long and narrow, some were short and wide. Will Haskell and Joseph Meeker decided to build a scow.

First they had to erect a log platform called

a saw pit. To make boards for their boat, they laid peeled logs on top of the platform and drew chalk lines along their sides. Then one of them stood on the platform, holding a six-foot saw by one handle. The other man stood under the platform, holding the other handle. Together they tried to saw along the chalk lines.

It was hard, back-breaking work. For two weeks they sawed boards. While they worked, they could hear the crash of falling trees in the hills, the rasp of saws, the pounding of mallets, and the shouts of other men working around them. It took another two weeks to

Half-built boats, mounds of supplies, and tents of all kinds share the crowded shores of Lake Bennett.

bend and hammer the boards together with wooden pegs to make their boat. But there was no hurry, for the ice did not start to leave the lake until almost the end of May. Most boats were ready in time.

By June 1 the lake was free of ice, and 7,124 boats had set sail on the green waters of Lake Bennett. It was a strange fleet indeed, with its rafts and dugouts, its scows and skiffs and punts. Some of the craft were fitted with sails and some were pushed along by oars or paddles. One boat had a crank that turned a pair of side paddle wheels.

52

Ahead of all of the *cheechakos* lay a long and dangerous voyage. First, they had to sail the length of Lake Bennett. From there they had to run through Miles Canyon, with its terrible rapids, to Lake Laberge. Then, after crossing Lake Laberge, they had to go down the Thirty-Mile River until they came to the upper Yukon River. A one-hundred-mile trip down this part of the Yukon would bring them at last to the gold fields.

Many of the people in the boats knew no more about handling them than they did about building them. Several of these strange craft,

These *cheechakos* travel in style as a tiny steamboat tows them down the Yukon River to the gold fields.

loaded with freight, tipped over as soon as they were put in the water. Others sank, and some leaked badly. But most of them were able to float across the calm waters of Lake Bennett.

When they reached Miles Canyon at the end of the lake, though, it was a different story. Here they had to go through Squaw Rapids and White Horse Rapids. Steep cliffs rose on both sides, and the river raced between them in white fury. In the first few days 150 boats were wrecked, and ten persons drowned in these raging waters. Many people lost their precious food and equipment and had to turn back without reaching their goal.

Flimsy boats and rafts were no match for the jagged rocks and racing waves of White Horse Rapids.

Will Haskell wrote about his trip through White Horse Rapids: "Here the water tumbled and tossed in most fantastic fashion, piling up spray in long, white columns ten or twelve feet high. Into the air we went and when the boat struck again, water flew over us in a torrent. We thought the next moment would see our boat sink but it didn't. I think it was the speed of the current that kept us afloat. At any rate, we reached shore safely but wet to the skin."

When they had passed through the rapids, Will Haskell and Joe Meeker had easier sailing for a time. They were able to enjoy the beautiful country through which they were traveling. Bluebells and lupin blossomed in great purple masses across the hills. Briar roses bloomed in the valleys, and blueberries, raspberries, and cranberries ripened among the rocks and mosses. Now and then a big moose walked out of a thicket, or a bear stood watching as they passed.

Along the way they passed villages of Stick Indians camped beside the river. They were catching great, silvery salmon, which they offered to sell to the *cheechakos* on their way to the Klondike.

"How muchee you pay? How muchee for salmon?" they shouted to the passengers in every boat.

Drifting down the swiftly flowing river, Will and Joe saw many interesting sights. There were always dozen of boats nearby and some of them carried strange cargoes. They saw one boat heaped with candy, lemons, oranges, and cucumbers which an Italian fruit dealer named Gandolfo was bringing to sell to the miners. They saw other boats filled with eggs. One boat carried 1,500 pairs of boots. Another carried a cow, and still another was loaded with chickens. But mostly the boats carried people hurrying to find gold in the Yukon.

After a week of sailing, Will and Joe came to Lake Laberge, where there was a Mounted Police station. They rowed across the lake and drifted on down the Thirty-Mile River. In this dangerous stretch they counted nineteen boats wrecked in the treacherous currents and they saw lonely wooden crosses on the shore, marking the graves of men who had drowned.

From here on it was smooth sailing again. After another week they glided into the mighty Yukon River and a few days later they rounded a rocky bluff. Here they had their first sight of the goal they had traveled so far and so long to reach.

On their right was the Klondike River thundering into the Yukon. Beyond it rose a big mountain. At its foot, spread along the banks of both rivers, were thousands of tents, shacks, partly finished hotels, sawmills, stores, dance halls, and shops. This was the new city of Dawson, not far from the mines on Bonanza and Eldorado Creeks. It had grown up as a result of the gold stampede and, for the next twelve months, it was to be the richest city in the North.

# 6.  A Dawson Store

On a pleasant July morning in 1898, Clarence Berry stood at the door of the Alaska Commercial Company store, looking out at the muddy main street of Dawson. It was called Front Street. He was very proud of this thriving city of tents and log cabins, frame houses, hotels, and shops, for he was one of its earliest settlers. He remembered when there had been nothing here but wilderness.

The city had been founded by Joseph Ladue,

a storekeeper of Fortymile. As soon as gold had been discovered on nearby Bonanza Creek, Ladue had built a sawmill here where the Klondike River flowed into the Yukon River. He knew that the *cheechakos* swarming here to look for gold would need lumber for sluice boxes. Others would want to build homes, churches, shops, hotels. And it had all come about as he had planned.

Thousands of people had poured into Dawson, and Joe Ladue had become a rich man. Anyone passing by the sawmill could still hear the screech of the saw as it ripped through pine logs and turned them into boards. But Ladue himself had returned to the United States the year before to live on his boyhood farm in New York.

The Alaska Commercial Company store was a big, square room with a counter running across the front and a pot-bellied stove in the corner. On one side were shelves stacked with flour, canned goods, sugar, tea, and other groceries. On the other side were racks of clothing. In front of the shelves were picks, shovels, guns, lanterns, miners' pans, tools, and dry goods. And there was a case filled with candy to be sold to the children.

Colorful signs and merchandise hang outside stores
tempting passersby on Front Street, Dawson, in 1898.

A person could buy almost anything he
wanted at this store. But everything was very
expensive because all the goods had to be
brought from the United States by steamship
and then by river boat up the Yukon River.
And the boats could only run in the summer
when the river was not frozen.

It was only eight o'clock in the morning, but
already the street was thronged with people.
Some were miners who had come to town from
their lonely cabins on the creeks. Some were
*cheechakos* who had just arrived in Dawson.
There were housewives, doctors, bakers, lawyers, sailors, children, carpenters. It was gold

60

that had brought them all to Dawson. All the men were tanned and many wore beards. Most were dressed in frayed, threadbare clothes, and it was hard to realize that some of them were worth a million dollars or more.

From where Berry stood he could see the tent where the *Klondike Nugget*, the Dawson newspaper, was published. The owner, Gene Allen, had carried his printing press, piece by piece, over White Pass. Then he had built a boat and floated the press to Dawson. Next door was the Presbyterian Church. It was made of logs and had rough planks for pews. The collection plate was a miner's pan, and

Food was more plentiful during the summer of 1898 when river boats brought supplies to Dawson.

the people put gold dust in it on Sundays. There were three other churches in Dawson: a Catholic Church, a Methodist Church, and an Anglican Church.

Near the Presbyterian Church was the Pavilion Dance Hall where there were square dances every night. A white-bearded fiddler played his violin and called out in a loud voice to the dancers:

"First two ladies cross over
    And by your opposites stand,
Second two ladies cross over
    And all join hands.
Now you form a circle
    With your backs against the wall,
Sashay to the center
    And promenade the hall."

The ladies wore their best taffeta and silk dresses, which had been carried all the way across the mountains, lakes, and rivers. The miners wore their newest red wool shirts and denim trousers. They also wore heavy cowhide boots. When they danced you could hear the *clump, clump* of these boots a block away.

Next door to the Pavilion Dance Hall was

the stand where Gandolfo, the Italian fruit
dealer, sold oranges for one dollar each.

The store began to fill with people. Some
of the miners were buying food to take back
to their cabins on the creeks. The *cheechakos*
were buying clothing, food, and equipment so
that they could go looking for gold. The
Alaska Commercial Company store was almost
like a club. The newcomers brought news of
the outside world, and the sourdoughs told
exciting stories of the gold fields.

The clerks treated all customers, *cheechakos* and old friends, alike. Those who had gold paid in dust for the goods they bought. But some of the men had no money at all. William Dietering and his partner, Joe Staley, had lost everything except the clothes they had on when their boat tipped over in White Horse Rapids. They needed food, clothing, and mining equipment. The clerk let them have everything they wanted. He wrote in a book a list of what they bought.

"You can pay me when you find gold," he said.

"But suppose we don't find any?" William Dietering asked.

"We'll take a chance," the clerk replied. "We've done the same for a lot of other men and some of them are millionaires today."

As William Dietering and Joe Staley were leaving the store, Big Alex McDonald walked in. Big Alex was a millionaire now, but he still wore a frayed wool shirt and faded corduroy trousers.

"Good morning," the tall miner said. "I need some grub."

A clerk took the list Big Alex gave him and went behind the counter. From the shelves he took beans, tea, flour, salt, bacon, canned milk, and sugar. The bill came to $40. Big Alex handed his deerskin bag of gold dust to the clerk. The clerk poured some of the dust onto his scales on the counter. It took two and one-half ounces of gold dust to equal $40. While the clerk weighed the gold dust, Big Alex looked out the window. The miners always did this because they believed that if you watched a man while he weighed your gold, it seemed as though you did not trust him.

The scales rested on a thick velvet cloth. Every week the clerks washed the cloth and saved the fine gold dust that had spilled on it when they weighed gold dust for their customers. Sometimes they washed $70 in gold dust from the cloth.

At all the shops the owners swept the floors and panned the dirt they picked up. It was always full of gold dust that had spilled from the miners' deerskin bags when they paid their bills. And when the owner of the Pavilion Dance Hall had his floor repaired, he panned $1,000 worth of gold dust from the ground beneath the floor, where it had sifted through the cracks.

# 7. A Busy Day

Robert Murray looked back up the dusty road and wished that his father and mother would hurry. For this was a very special day. Early that morning he and his parents had left their cabin on Bonanza Creek to go to Dawson more than ten miles away. They had all left together, but Robert had hurried on ahead. This was the first time he had been to the city in eight months and he could hardly wait to get there.

He knew that this was a happy outing for his mother and father, too. His mother wanted to visit her friend, Mrs. Wills. His father had business to attend to and provisions to buy at the Alaska Commercial Company store. And Robert wanted to see the sights. He was ten years old and had lived all his life in the North. Ever since his father had found gold on Bonanza Creek, the Murrays had lived in a cabin near their mine.

Robert stopped to pick a handful of salmonberries beside the road, and soon he could see his parents coming around the bend. His father was leading Old Jess, the pack horse. Strapped to Old Jess's back were two sacks containing 180 pounds of gold dust. This was the gold his father had dug from his mine during the past four months. It was worth $46,000, and he was taking it to the Bank of British North America. He did not fear carrying so much gold, for there was no robbery in the Yukon. The Mounted Police had seen to that. You could leave your cabin unlocked the year round, and no one would touch anything.

Many people were on the road this morning. There were miners going to and from Dawson. There were *cheechakos* going back into the hills to look for gold. There were Mounted Police-

Roadhouses like *The Magnet* provided refreshments
and good times for miners and their families.

men, loggers, hunters carrying small game to
market, and Indians. Some carried gold or
provisions on their backs, and one man was
pushing a wheelbarrow loaded with sacks of
gold dust. As the Murrays came nearer to
Dawson, the number of people on the road
increased. Then they rounded a curve and saw
the first tents and log houses of the city.

Soon they were walking past the shops and
restaurants, the hotels, saloons, and dance halls
crowded together on both sides of muddy
Front Street. Bright-colored banners and signs
hung in front of these buildings. Signs like

these told what was for sale or what went on inside:

Gold Dust Bought and Sold    Good Meals
Bakery    Patent Medicines    Bed and Board
Teeth Filled and Pulled    Cigars
Nugget Saloon    Fresh Fish and Moose Meat

New buildings were going up everywhere. Dawson continued to grow.

The Murrays went first to the Bank of British North America. It occupied a tent and had a plank for a counter and an old trunk for a safe. The trunk was filled with bills, and the floor was piled high with sacks of gold. People exchanged their gold for paper money here.

Miners and townsfolk throng Front Street in summer.

They deposited the paper money in the bank, but for spending money, nearly everyone preferred gold dust.

From the bank the Murrays went to the store. Here Robert's father bought food and equipment to take back to their cabin. He also bought a sack of peppermint candy for Robert and ten yards of brown woolen cloth for a new dress for Mrs. Murray.

Then Mr. Murray went to see William Ogilvie, the government surveyor. Mrs. Murray and Robert went to the neat log cabin where Mrs. Wills lived. She was a widow and she earned some money by baking bread, which she sold at a dollar a loaf. Usually she baked more than 30 loaves a day.

Mrs. Wills also owned a gold mine on Eldorado Creek. With the money she had made from selling bread she had hired men to work in her mine. People said her mine had paid her $12,000 in one month this summer, but she still baked bread almost every day in her big wood stove.

She gave Robert two thick slices, still warm from the oven, and spread with wild strawberry jam. While his mother and Mrs. Wills chatted, Robert set out to see the sights.

As he passed a big frame house, a pair of husky puppies, looking like small white balls of wool, waddled over to him. Robert knew that this was the home of the wealthy man named Jim Daugherty and the puppies belonged to him. When they grew up, they would be sled dogs like their parents.

There were many dogs in Dawson—strong, well-trained dogs, used to pulling the heavily loaded sleds over ice and through deep snow. Some of these sled dogs were expensive. Robert had heard that Jim Daugherty's team of eight husky dogs was worth $2,500 and he fed

Dog teams were best for long trips in the Klondike. Good dogs could pull heavy loads eight hours a day.

them several thousands of pounds of bacon and fish each year.

He admired the puppies tumbling about near his feet. Suddenly, in the distance, he heard a hoarse bellowing sound.

"Steamboat coming!" someone shouted.

Turning quickly, Robert ran after the crowd hurrying down to the river. When he got there, the steamboat *Alice* was just gliding up to the dock with her stern paddle wheel chuffing and thrashing the water to foam. The *Alice*'s deck was jammed with passengers waving and shouting to the throng on the dock, who waved and shouted back.

"Hurrah for the gold!" the people on the *Alice* shouted. "Show us the gold!"

"What's the news?" the people on the dock shouted back. "How are things in the United States?"

As the newcomers swarmed ashore, the crew started unloading the *Alice*'s cargo. She had brought tons of food, champagne, cigars, dry goods, hardware, and kerosene oil for the shops

Clerks pose with one and a half tons of gold bricks and dust awaiting shipment to the United States.

and the restaurants of Dawson. When she left again, her hold would be filled with gold bars and gold dust bound for the United States.

Robert followed the crowd back to bustling Front Street. There was so much to see— jewelry and guns, fishing rods, cakes, toys, furs, Indian curios, harnesses, and a live black bear doing a shuffling dance while his master played on a harmonica. Robert hated to leave this exciting street, which was like a big fair. But he knew his parents would be expecting him, so in the late afternoon he went back to Mrs. Wills's house.

When his father came in, Mrs. Wills gave them a supper of moose steaks and beans with some of her freshly baked bread. Then they started the long walk back to their cabin on Bonanza Creek. Robert was tired as he trudged up the road behind Old Jess. But he didn't care, for it had been a wonderful day.

# 8. The Big Spenders

In July 1898, Dawson was just a careless collection of tents, shacks, and small log buildings. But by July 1899, it had become a big city. It had telephones, running water, steam heat, and electricity in some buildings. It had big houses, good restaurants, an opera house, dozens of shops, and two hospitals. People called it the "San Francisco of the North." Dawson had been built by gold, and some of its citizens were among the wealthiest men in America. These were the lucky miners who had found gold along Bonanza and Eldorado Creeks.

Pack mules loaded with gold dust and nuggets were a common sight in Dawson in 1899.

One of the richest of them was Big Alex McDonald. With the money from his first mine on Eldorado Creek, he bought more mines until he owned 50. From one mine he took $20,000 worth of gold in a single day. His fifteen-mule pack train loaded with gold was seen often on the road to Dawson. He had workmen make him a large building, which he named The McDonald, and where he lived like a king. He kept a bowl of gold nuggets on the sideboard and when visitors came, he told them:

"Help yourself to some nuggets. There are plenty more where these came from."

Big Alex also traveled a great deal. He

went to Rome, Paris, and London, where he stayed at the finest hotels.

Another wealthy man was Thomas Lippy, who took more than two million dollars from his mine, Sixteen Above, on Eldorado Creek. Another millionaire was Clarence Berry. He still lived in his tiny cabin on Eldorado. He had the only cow in the area and could drink fresh milk every day. But it was expensive, for he had to pay $400 a ton for hay to feed his cow. Like Big Alex McDonald, he gave away nuggets. He kept a bucket of them on a post in front of his cabin. On it was a sign, "Help Yourself."

Still another Klondike millionaire was William Gates, nicknamed Swiftwater Bill. He was a short, wiry man with bright blue eyes and a little pointed beard. He had once been a poor man. Then he had bought a share in a gold mine on Bonanza Creek. The mine proved to be rich, and soon Swiftwater Bill could buy shares in other mines. When he became wealthy, he enjoyed going to the theater in Dawson, dressed up in a Prince Albert coat, with a big diamond stickpin in his tie.

Claim Number Twenty-Nine Above, next to Big Alex McDonald's mine, was owned by a

Swede named Charles Anderson. People called him the Lucky Swede because he had paid a man $800 for this mine, which was, at first, thought to be worthless. Then he dug more than a million dollars worth of gold from it.

One of the luckiest men in the gold rush was Richard Lowe. He had been a mule driver in the West before he went to the Yukon. There he became a helper to the government surveyor, William Ogilvie. It was Ogilvie's job to measure all the miners' claims and to see that they were not more than 500 feet long. Richard Lowe carried the surveyor's chain and held the stake while Ogilvie measured.

Sometimes the miners had not measured accurately, and there would be too many feet of land in their claims. Other people could claim these extra feet of land if they wanted to. One day Ogilvie found that claim Two Above on Eldorado was too long on one side. It had a pie-shaped piece of ground that was extra, 86 feet wide at its broadest point.

No one knew whether there was any gold in this piece of land. But Lowe decided to claim it. At first he tried to sell his new claim for $900, but no one would buy it. So he decided to dig a mine there himself. When he hit the pay streak, he took $46,000 from his mine in eight hours. It turned out to be the richest piece of ground of its size ever discovered. Now Lowe was very wealthy. He lived in a fine house in Dawson and drove a shiny carriage behind a pair of beautiful black horses. The horses had gold nuggets in their harnesses.

Not all the people who became millionaires were men. Some women also made fortunes in the gold fields. One of them was Belinda Mulroney, a coal miner's daughter from Scranton, Pennsylvania. She went to Alaska as a stewardess on the steamship *City of Topeka*. When she heard about the Klondike gold rush, she bought a lot of dresses and hot water bottles. She carried them over Chilkoot Pass with the help of two Indians and floated them down the river to Dawson on a raft.

With the money she made from selling the dresses and hot water bottles, she started a restaurant. With the money she made from the restaurant, she bought shares in gold mines. When she had enough money, she built the biggest and finest hotel in Dawson. She called it the Fairview.

There were 22 steam-heated rooms in the Fairview with electric lights and hot and cold

running water. The tables in the dining room
were spread with linen cloths, sterling silver,
and fine china. All the furnishings, from beds
to cut-glass chandeliers, had been carried over
White Pass on the Dead Horse Trail and then
floated down the river on fifteen scows.

On the first day the new hotel was in business, Belinda Mulroney took in thousands of
dollars. The hotel restaurant was a favorite
dining place for Big Alex McDonald, Swiftwater Bill Gates, the Lucky Swede, and other
Klondike kings. At the Fairview one could
dine on oysters, lobster, little French cakes

called *petits fours*, and other good dishes prepared by fine chefs. But it was expensive. Here is a bill for a dinner at the Fairview Hotel:

| | |
|---|---:|
| 1 can Eastern oysters for two . . . . . . | $15.00 |
| 1 roast duck for two . . . | 6.00 |
| 2 porterhouse moose steaks . | 5.00 |
| 1 pint bottle of champagne . | 30.00 |
| | $56.00 |

When the diners had finished eating, they would hand their deerskin bags to the waiter. He took them to the cashier, who weighed out enough gold dust to pay for the meal. Before putting their bags in their pockets, the diners always left a pinch of gold dust on a plate as the waiter's tip.

# 9. The End of the Gold Rush

In the spring of 1899 people thought that Dawson would always be a big and important city. But certain events would soon bring an end to its short career as the "San Francisco of the North" and to the Klondike gold rush as well.

On the night of April 26, 1899, a fire broke out in a dance hall on Front Street. The temperature was 46 degrees below zero, and water froze in the firemen's hoses. While people

watched helplessly, showering sparks spread
the fire from building to building. Dry wooden
shops and stores exploded into flames that
licked and towered skyward through a dense
curtain of smoke. The opera house, the Bank
of British North America, and the Pavilion
Dance Hall were destroyed, together with 117
other buildings. The loss came to more than
one million dollars.

The entire city might have been consumed
if it had not been for Captain Cortlandt Starnes
of the Mounted Police. He had his men use
dynamite to blow up some of the buildings in

the path of the fire. This kept the flames from spreading beyond Front Street.

Many of the burned buildings were replaced, but somehow Dawson was never the same again. Other things had also changed. Although a number of very wealthy people lived in Dawson, a great many more people were poor and getting poorer. Most of the wealthy people were the men and women who had been on hand when gold was discovered on Bonanza Creek. They had been the first to arrive and they had staked the best claims. Only a few of the thousands of *cheechakos* who swarmed into the Yukon to look for gold had found any.

The rest had kept searching until their supplies and their money and their hopes were gone. Then, discouraged, they had turned to other work. Some found jobs in other men's mines. Some became clerks in stores, waiters in restaurants, dock workers, or carpenters. But there were so many of these people that there were not enough jobs to go around. Wages dropped from $15 to about $3.00 a day. And $3.00 would buy very little in a city where

As gold claims became scarce, newcomers to the gold fields had to work for other miners at low wages.

butter cost $1.00 a pound, condensed milk 50 cents a can, and shoes $10 a pair.

And people began to worry about the winter that lay ahead. When the river froze, no more steamboats could sail to Dawson with food. During the past winter, food had become very scarce. The coming winter might even bring starvation. Fearing this, a number of people who could afford to pay for their passage decided to take a steamer back to the United States while there was still time.

Then in the late summer rumors began to reach Dawson about a great new gold strike on Norton Sound in Alaska, near the mouth of the Yukon River. And just as men had left Fortymile three years before to go to Bonanza Creek, people began leaving Dawson for the new gold fields. They went first by twos and then by dozens.

Soon word came back that the rumors were true. Fortunes were being made around Nome, Alaska. A tent city was springing up near the beach there. Log houses were going up, along with dance halls, churches, restaurants, and stores. Men were staking claims and digging shafts, just as they had done in the Klondike.

A great wave of excitement swept through

Dawson, and a stampede for the new gold fields began. Men who had fought their way over the mountains and down the river to Dawson now feverishly joined the race to Nome. Perhaps this time they would find gold. Cabins were left deserted as steamer after steamer with crowded decks took off for Nome. In one week alone, 8,000 people left Dawson. Soon there were few customers left in the stores and dance halls. The dining room in Belinda Mulroney's Fairview Hotel was almost empty.

A few of the wealthy miners who had found gold on Bonanza and Eldorado Creek stayed on for a time in Dawson. But even they were

A few guests pose in front of the Fairview in almost deserted Dawson in 1904.

growing tired of the cold Yukon winters. Some of those who had come from the United States returned home. They built fine houses in Seattle and San Francisco. Tom Lippy was one of these men. George Carmack and his wife drove about Seattle in a carriage with a sign: *George Carmack, Discoverer Of Gold In The Klondike.* Then Carmack moved to a big house in Vancouver, Washington.

By early fall, the "San Francisco of the North" had turned into a ghost town. The great Klondike gold rush had ended as suddenly as it had begun.

But its effects were lasting. If it had not been for the Klondike gold rush, Alaska might perhaps have remained a vast wilderness. As it was, the men who came to the Klondike to look for gold moved on to settle Nome. From there they spread out to Fairbanks and Atlin, where other gold discoveries were made.

Men found, too, that there were other riches besides gold in Alaska. Prospectors looking for the yellow metal discovered copper, lead, cobalt, silver, uranium, and oil. Today, Alaska sends us large quantities of these mineral products. Great dredges and electrical machinery have taken the place of the shovels and pans and sluice boxes of the old-time miners.

A number of men who had been unable to find gold made fortunes in the lumber, fur, and salmon of Alaska. Thriving towns grew up around the mines and lumber mills and salmon canneries. The children and grandchildren of the miners of 1898 stayed on in Alaska to raise their families and to build more towns. Railroads and highways opened up the country so that people could travel more easily for business and pleasure. In more recent times the airplane has brought lonely mining towns and lumber camps closer to civilization. Today one can travel by air in an hour to places which it took the gold-rush *cheechakos* weeks to reach in former times.

This new ease and speed of travel brought thousands of tourists to see the sights of Alaska, its snow-capped mountains and wooded valleys and great glaciers. The tourist business brought new money to Alaska. In 1959, Alaska became our 49th and our largest state. And perhaps it all came about because on a hot August afternoon in 1896, George Carmack and his friends, Skookum Jim and Tagish Charlie, discovered gold on Rabbit Creek.

# Glossary

*cheechako*: an Indian word which means greenhorn or tenderfoot

**Chilkoot lockstep**: walking in tight formation up the steepest section of the Chilkoot Pass

**claim**: an area of land marked off by a miner as his own

**drift**: a tunnel from a mine shaft into or along the path of a vein of gold

**drifting**: digging a horizontal tunnel into or along the path of a vein of gold

**"lone wolf"**: the term used by miners to describe one who mined gold without any partners

**mother lode**: the largest deposit of ore in a region

**pay streak**: a rich vein of gold usually located twenty or thirty feet underground

**prospector**: one who searches for deposits of gold or other metals

**saw pit**: a pit over which timber is sawed by a long, two-handled saw operated by two men

**scow**: a large flat-bottomed boat with square ends, used to carry freight

**shaft**: a long, narrow opening or passage dug into the earth for mining purposes

**sluice box**: an open-ended wooden box

**sluice line**: a series of sluice boxes which are fitted together to make a long channel. Water rushing through the sluice line separates gold from dirt.

**sourdough**: fermented dough which is added to a new batch of dough to make it rise; a nickname for miners

**stake**: to mark the location of boundaries of an area one wishes to mine

**windlass**: a machine for hoisting or pulling

93

# Index